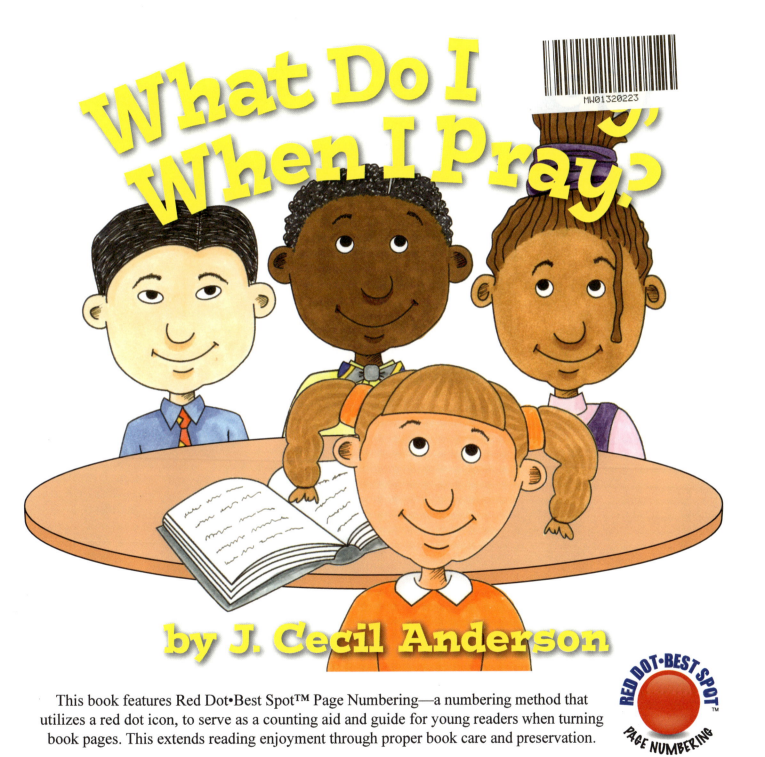

What Do I Say, When I Pray?

by J. Cecil Anderson

This book features Red Dot•Best Spot™ Page Numbering—a numbering method that utilizes a red dot icon, to serve as a counting aid and guide for young readers when turning book pages. This extends reading enjoyment through proper book care and preservation.

Written, illustrated and designed by J. Cecil Anderson

What Do I Say, When I Pray?
ISBN 978-0-615-33948-1

©2009 J. Cecil Anderson
All rights reserved. Any reproduction, republication, or other use of all or part of any contents of this book is expressly prohibited, unless prior written permission has been granted by the author. All names, logos, slogans, and trademarks that appear in this book may not be used in any advertising, publicity, promotion, or in any other manner implying endorsement, sponsorship of, or affiliation with any product or service, without prior written permission of the author.

Scriptures are from the *Holy Bible* (King James Version).

**P.O. Box 954
Fairburn, Georgia 30213**

Manufactured in the U.S.A.

Dedication

To Father God, for your extraordinary gifts and the opportunity to use them
in such an awesome ministry. Be glorified and magnified in all I do!

To my wonderful wife: Your continual support keeps me motivated and focused.
I love you dearly. God has so much more in store and I am glad
we get to experience it all together.

To Mom for teaching me Godly character and
to Dad for showing me relentless determination.

To my late grandfather Deacon Henry Anderson for
speaking forth God's will over me at birth. To God be the glory!

Acknowledgments

My sincere thanks to everyone who has contributed to, and supported, this ministry.
I pray Father God's blessings to you are exceedingly great.

Dear Friend,

Enjoy learning how to talk to Father God.

Happy Reading!

J. Geri C.

I think my parents are really great.
I am happy they are mine to keep.

They show me lots of love and care,
and they **tuck** me in to sleep.

When we wake up in the morning,
we give thanks for all God has done.

We get dressed, then have some breakfast,
and now our day has begun.

We spend plenty of time together, and all laugh and giggle a lot.

Now we are on our way to church, and that is my favorite **spot**.

All of my best friends will be there.
You know! Joey, Sara, and Mike.

Today I get to read our study **scripture**,
and that I really, really like.

On the way home I had a thought.
There is something that I remember.

The day my parents had their **wedding** is coming up in December.

The *Bible* teaches if I show them **honor**,
I will live long and be **blessed** every day.

So I want to buy them a special gift,
but I have no money to pay.

I know! I will **pray** to Father God for help.
I am sure this He will gladly do.

I learned this in our children's church,
how He loves my parents, me and you too.

Mike said, "Ummm, I do not know, because God lives past the moon."

Joey said, "Why not talk to Him now?
Just speak up right away.

When I need to talk with Father God,
I just bow my head and pray."

"But what do I say, when I pray?
Which words would be the best?

Do I use small ones or really big ones,
like those from a spelling test?"

"Use what we read in the *Bible*.
That would make God very proud.

He knows each and every word,"
Sara gladly said out loud.

"The *Bible* is the words of God,"
Mike thought and said with a grin.

"My Pa Pa taught me about that lesson,
and how God's **promises** are all within."

"This is great!
I will use a scripture,
and one like this would
do just fine.

It says God will give me all that I need,
which is perfect for a **task** like mine."

Philippians 4:19
But my God shall supply all your need according to his riches in glory by Christ Jesus.

"Thanks, my friends. You are the best!
You helped me find what to say.

I know Father God will help me,
because I know just what to pray."

Praying What God Says

The *Holy Bible* is a book of sacred writings that God provided for people so that they could live a **holy**, purposeful life. It was written many years ago by men who loved and obeyed God. It is filled with information about God, people, places, and events. The *Bible* contains the words of God. His words are scriptures that we can use when we pray. Some scriptures are promises to anyone who accepts Jesus Christ as their **Saviour**—and Father God always keeps His promises. By studying God's Word and thinking about it every day, we can learn to pray what God says.

Some scriptures we can say when we pray:

Confidence (in Him)
I John 5:14,15 And this is the confidence that we have in him, that, if we ask any thing according to his will, he heareth us: And if we know that he hear us, whatsoever we ask, we know that we have the petitions that we desired of him.

Eternal Life (in Heaven)
John 3:16 For God so loved the world, that he gave his only begotten Son, that whosoever believeth in him should not perish, but have everlasting life.

Wisdom and Guidance
Psalm 32:8 I will instruct thee and teach thee in the way which thou shalt go: I will guide thee with mine eye.

Forgiveness
1 John 1:9 If we confess our sins, he is faithful and just to forgive us our sins, and to cleanse us from all unrighteousness.

Peace
Isaiah 26:3 Thou wilt keep him in perfect peace, whose mind is stayed on thee: because he trusteth in thee.

Safety and Protection
Psalm 91:4 He shall cover thee with his feathers, and under his wings shalt thou trust: his truth shall be thy shield and buckler.

Health
Proverbs 4:20,22 My son, attend to my words; incline thine ear unto my sayings. For they are life unto those that find them, and health to all their flesh.

Long Life (on Earth)
Ephesians 6:2,3 Honour thy father and mother; which is the first commandment with promise; That it may be well with thee, and thou mayest live long on the earth.

Words To Grow On

anniversary: a date people remember because something important happened on that date in the past

blessed: to have favor and approval from Father God

holy: to be dedicated for the service of Father God

honor: to show or have great respect for someone

pray: to ask something of Father God in a humble way

promise: a pledge given by someone that something will be done

Saviour: He (Jesus Christ) who saves people from the power and punishment of sin

scripture: sacred writings from the *Holy Bible*

spot: a place that is interesting or a special location

task: something to be done; a job or duty

tuck: to put to bed and cover snugly

wedding: a marriage ceremony between a man and a woman

Empowering generations... for greatness.™

www.holychildbooks.com

CPSIA information can be obtained
at www.ICGtesting.com
Printed in the USA
237460LV00001B